The Victory of the Cross

A Passion Play

M. Creagh-Henry

A SAMUEL FRENCH ACTING EDITION

SAMUEL FRENCH

FOUNDED 1830

SAMUELFRENCH-LONDON.CO.UK
SAMUELFRENCH.COM

ISBN 978-0-573-06250-6

www.samuelfrench-london.co.uk

www.samuelfrench.com

FOR AMATEUR PRODUCTION ENQUIRIES

UNITED KINGDOM AND WORLD
EXCLUDING NORTH AMERICA
plays@SamuelFrench-London.co.uk
020 7255 4302/01

Each title is subject to availability from Samuel French,

depending upon country of performance.

CHARACTERS

THE BLESSED VIRGIN MARY

RACHEL, *a disciple*

ANNA, *a beggar woman*

MARY MAGDALEN

JOHN

PETER

JUDAS

SYNOPSIS OF SCENES

A room in the House where the Last Supper took place.

SCENE 1: Maundy Thursday.

SCENE 2: Good Friday morning.

SCENE 3: Easter morning, early.

THE VICTORY OF THE CROSS

SCENE I

(MAUNDY THURSDAY)

SCENE: *A room in the house where the Last Supper took place. There are two doorways, one up R., leading to the street, and one in the L. wall, leading to the inner part of the house. C. in the back wall is a window. A table and two stools comprise the furniture. Two jars stand on the table.*

(See the GROUND PLAN at the end of the play.)

When the CURTAIN rises RACHEL is seated on the stool R. grinding corn with a pestle and mortar. MARY, the Mother of Jesus, enters L.

MARY. The Upper Room is empty. Jesus and the disciples left the house when they had eaten the Passover.

RACHEL. I was at the window and saw them go, singing the Paschal Psalm as they took the road up to the Mount of Olives.

MARY. To the Garden of Gethsemane, the garden Jesus loves. (*She comes* C.) There He finds rest and peace after a long day of healing the sick and preaching His Gospel of Love.

RACHEL. He went before the disciples, like a shepherd leading His flock, but only eleven followed him, one was missing.

MARY. Sent on some errand of mercy no doubt. (*She sits on the stool* L. *and picks up a small piece of cross-stitch which is lying on the table, and works.*)

1

RACHEL. It is late for errands, even errands of mercy.

MARY. Jesus is never limited by time, so long as any need Him He is there, to help or heal.

RACHEL. I know that only too well! How often have I prepared meals, which He has never eaten, because He would not leave the crowds which thronged Him, waiting to be healed. (*She rises and crosses to the table. She pours the corn she has ground into a jar and takes a handful from another jar for grinding.*) All day long he has stayed tending them.

MARY (*smiling*). Poor Rachel! But He came in at last, and enjoyed the meal you had prepared.

RACHEL. By that time it was spoiled! (*She comes above the table.*) Yet how could I be vexed when He thanked me with that radiant smile of His, and asked me to forgive him. What is it about Jesus which so attracts people ?

MARY. His friendliness, the Spirit of Love, which shines through Him. See how at His call, the disciples at once left all to follow him.

RACHEL. He demands much of His followers. (*She crosses to the stool* R. *and sits, grinding again.*)

MARY. He demands *all*, and they were ready to give it.

RACHEL. It must have rejoiced them to see how wildly the people welcomed the Master when He entered Jerusalem.

MARY. What is the shouting of a crowd worth ? It is unstable and apt to change from one day to the next. . . . I cannot overcome a sense of fear, Rachel.

RACHEL. What can you have to fear ?

MARY. It is a vague and shadowy fear. The people's welcome of Jesus angered the priests and Pharisees. Then his first act on entering the city was to clear the Temple of its bartering crowd. That was a bold deed.

RACHEL. I was there and saw the scene. It was grand! All the beasts for sacrifice were standing in the Temple court, the oxen lowing, the sheep bleating, it was like a cattle market. Jesus stood in the middle of it, His eyes flashing with anger. Then His voice rang out above the noise—" It is written My house is the house of prayer, but you have made it a den of thieves."

MARY. I can picture His anger.

RACHEL. He drove the beasts out of the Temple court. Then, as He passed the tables of the money-changers, He threw them over and all their money rolled upon the ground. I laughed to see them scrambling for the coins. The priests and Pharisees were angry it is true, but Jesus has no fear.

MARY. None; but I fear for him.

(There is knocking at the street door.)

ANNA *(off)*. May I come in ? I am hurt.

MARY. See who is in need of help, Rachel.

*(*RACHEL *rises and exits* R. *She returns almost immediately supporting a woman—*ANNA*—who limps, one foot being injured.* MARY *rises and goes forward to meet her.)*

ANNA. There was a light in your house, all the others were dark, so I came to your door.

MARY *(leading her to the stool,* R.*)*. You are welcome. How did you hurt your foot ?

ANNA *(sitting)*. I fell, and it turned under me.

*(*MARY *kneels before* ANNA, *down* L. *of her, and removes the sandal from her left foot. She takes the foot gently and examines it.)*

MARY. Fetch a basin of water and a towel, Rachel.

*(*RACHEL *exits* L.*)*

No bone is broken, but the foot is sprained. We will bathe it and the pain will soon go. *(She manipulates the foot.)*

ANNA.   Your hands are so gentle.

(RACHEL *enters, with a basin of water and a towel and sponge. She crosses and puts them beside* MARY, *who commences to bathe the woman's foot, and manipulates it.*)

RACHEL.   How did you come to fall ?
ANNA.   A man in the crowd pushed me, and I stumbled and fell.
RACHEL. The crowd—where could there be a crowd at this hour of night ?
ANNA.   At the end of this street. Did you not hear the soldiers marching ?
RACHEL.   I did hear soldiers, and wondered what they were doing so late, but why should a crowd follow them ?
ANNA.   They went out armed to take some thief I heard.   So all who were abroad tonight followed, to see him arrested.
RACHEL.   A thief should not need a company of soldiers to capture him.
ANNA.   But they said he had a band of robbers with him, dangerous men. I was asleep in a doorway when the noise of the crowd woke me. I joined it when they came back, that is when I fell, so I did not see him.
MARY.   You were asleep in a doorway—Have you no home ?
ANNA.   No, Lady, I have no home . . . I have nothing. . . . nothing. I was ugly and no man asked me in marriage, so when my parents died, I was left alone and penniless. Now I sit on the Temple steps all day with my beggar's bowl—and think.

(MARY *hands the basin to* RACHEL *and dries* ANNA'S
foot.)

RACHEL.   What do you think about.
ANNA.   Nothing.

RACHEL (*moving up to the table with the basin*). It is surely impossible to think of nothing.

ANNA. What have I to think of? If I thought of anything it could only be of cold and hunger and death . . . cruel ugly things . . . dread things . . . things I fear.

(RACHEL *turns and puts the basin on the table.*)

MARY. Fear is a devil, which may be cast out by faith and prayer. We should pray to God as to a father, who cares for all His children, so we say:— " Our Father, who art in Heaven."

ANNA. Our Father! That brings Him very near . . . If I may speak so simply to Jehovah, I will ask Him to cast out my fear.

MARY (*putting on* ANNA'S *sandal*). And He will do so. . . . See now if your foot is better. (*She rises.*)

ANNA (*moving her foot; then crying joyfully*). The pain is gone! (*She rises, tries her weight on the foot then crosses down* L.) See! See! I can walk, my foot is healed. . . . Oh, I am grateful to you, Lady.

MARY. The power healed you.

ANNA. What power?

MARY. Faith. The Faith through which God works; though he may use human hands to do His work.

RACHEL. Jesus says Faith can work miracles.

ANNA. Do you mean Jesus—the prophet from Nazareth?

RACHEL. Yes. Who else could I mean?

ANNA. *I hate him.*

(MARY *turns away.*)

RACHEL (*furiously*). Woman! Do you know who—

MARY (*instantly*). Peace Rachel! (*To* ANNA.) Why do you say that? You cannot know him.

ANNA. No, I do not know him. I have never even seen him, but he came to the Temple yesterday and

*

made a terrible scene, driving out all the animals, and upsetting the tables of the money-changers. Those who go up daily to pray or offer sacrifice, drop money in my bowl as they return, but he had frightened them so much by his anger, that they all ran away down the Temple steps so I had not one coin in my bowl, not a penny to buy food. It was *his* fault—that is why I hate him. (*She moves up to the window and looks out.*)

RACHEL (*crossing to* MARY). O Mary. How dare she say that! How dare she!

MARY. Do not be angry, Rachel. Try to understand and pity her.

RACHEL. If *you* can forgive, I surely must . . . but it is not easy.

(ANNA *looks out of the window for a few moments watching tensely.*)

MARY. Look. . . . How tensely she is watching something.

(ANNA *turns, but remains up stage, standing with a rapt expression, looking above and beyond* MARY. RACHEL *watches her for a moment. Then she goes up and leans out of the window, looking off* R.)

(*To* ANNA.) Something has moved you strangely. What have you seen ?

ANNA (*speaking slowly as if in a dream*). A man's face in the moonlight.

MARY. A man's face ?

ANNA. Yes. (*She comes down slowly towards* MARY.) A face, strong and suffering, with deep compassion in his eyes. . . . He seemed to look right into my soul.

MARY. There were others with Him, were there not ?

ANNA. Yes—there were others—but he looked up at this window as he passed, the rest became as shadows. . . . I only saw *his* face.

RACHEL (*turning down stage*). The man you saw was Jesus of Nazareth.

ANNA (*quietly*). Jesus of Nazareth. It was Jesus of Nazareth. I have seen Him. (*Her gaze returns to* MARY'S *face*.) There is something about His face . . . the tenderness in His eyes, I think, which I see in your own.

MARY. I am his Mother.

ANNA. His mother! (*She throws herself on her knees*.) O Lady, forgive me. . . . Forgive my mad and wicked words. I did not know—

MARY (*holding out her hands and rasing* ANNA). I forgive you—as He would. You spoke in ignorance.

ANNA. O Blessed Mother of Blessed Son . . . From my heart I thank you for your goodness and forgiveness. God must have guided me to this house. Now I go. It is late and you must be weary.

MARY. You cannot go out to sleep in a doorway, stay with us until your foot is strong again.

ANNA. Stay with you, Lady! I—a beggar—a stranger—

RACHEL (*coming above the table*). Jesus once said— I was a stranger and you took Me in. " If you have done it to one of the least of these you have done it to Me."

MARY. It would be my Son's will that you should remain with us.

ANNA. Lady, how can I thank you ? I am grateful indeed.

RACHEL. Come. (*She picks up the basin and crosses to the doorway* L.) Sleep here in peace.

(*She exits.* ANNA *follows her to the doorway, then she pauses and says—*)

ANNA. Our Father, who art in Heaven—I thank thee.

(*She exits.* MARY *crosses to the stool* L., *sits and takes up her work.* RACHEL *enters.*)

RACHEL.   She learns quickly.

MARY.   Those who are in need of comfort make apt pupils, Rachel.

RACHEL.   When I saw Jesus from the window just now, He was walking with soldiers.

MARY.   With soldiers!   How strange!   I thought He would have been with the disciples.

(*Enter* MARY MAGDALEN, R.   *She stands silent at* R.C., *with bowed head.*)

MARY (*rising*).   Mary, what brings you here so late ?

MAGDALEN.   They have arrested Jesus.

MARY.   Arrested my son!

RACHEL.   Arrested Jesus!   Where did you hear this ?

MAGDALEN.   I *felt* there was danger coming to the Master.   I had heard of secret meetings of scribes and elders with the priests, so I watched tonight near the house of the High Priest and saw their guard set out, soon followed by a rabble from the streets.   I joined the crowd and we went up to the Mount of Olives.

MARY.   To the Garden of Gethsemane ?

MAGDALEN.   Yes, Lady. . . . Jesus was there.   He stood quiet and unafraid, waiting for his enemies, as though he expected them.

MARY.   In his Garden of Peace!   Were not His disciples with Him ?

MAGDALEN.   A few stood near, but what was most strange, the soldiers were led by one of them.

MARY.   That could not be!   Not one of his chosen band would ever fail him.

MAGDALEN.   Alas!   I have sure proof—one of the twelve disciples is a traitor.

MARY.   What is your proof ?

MAGDALEN.   The man who led the guard went forward and kissed Jesus.   In the light of the torches I could see the Master's sorrowful face.   " Judas, betrayest thou the Son of Man with a kiss ? " he said.

MARY. Judas! His Disciple!

MAGDALEN. Peter, with a sword, struck off the ear of a soldier who held the Master, but Jesus touched the wound, and it was healed.

RACHEL. Who but He would show an enemy such compassion!

MAGDALEN. A soldier raised a leaded whip to strike Jesus—I ran forward and caught his arm. He turned furiously and struck me instead. (*She turns back her sleeve*.) See. . . . I rejoice that I have borne one stripe for him.

RACHEL. It is a cruel stripe indeed.

MARY. Did Jesus speak ?

MAGDALEN. He said—"Are you come as against a thief with swords and staves ? When I was daily with you, you stretched out no hand against Me, but this is your hour and the power of darkness."

MARY. It is their hour and the power of darkness indeed.

MAGDALEN. Oh! *Why* does He surrender himself to that evil power ? (*To* MARY.) And *you* must face the hour of darkness, too.

MARY. Shall I not share it with Him to the uttermost ? (*She crosses down* R.)

(*Enter* JOHN *hurriedly* R., *he senses the tense atmosphere looks at the women and realises they have heard of the arrest.*)

JOHN. You have already heard the news I bring ?

MARY. We have heard it.

MAGDALEN. I was in the Garden of Gethsemane.

JOHN. From there the Master was taken to the house of the High Priest.

MARY. Were you with Him ?

JOHN. I was in the Court and heard all their false witness, but the witnesses contradicted each other. The High Priest bade the Master tell him of his new doctrine. Jesus replied " I spoke openly to the world, I taught in the synagogues and have held no secret meeting. Why do you ask Me ? Ask those who heard Me what I said to them." At that, an officer who stood by, struck Jesus on the mouth.

MAGDALEN.   How dare they strike Him ? Could you do nothing ?

JOHN (*turning to* MAGDALEN).   What could I do in the High Priest's Court ? I who in Gethsemane had fled, afraid!   With bitter shame I confess it!   We all forsook Him there! (*He turns away ashamed and moves up* R., *his back to audience.*)

MARY.   You all forsook Him!

MAGDALEN.   I remember—not one of His Disciples was beside Him when He was led away. The friends He trusted!   Cowards—all of you!

MARY.   Peace, Mary.   Continue, John, is there more to tell ?

JOHN (*turning*).   The priests and elders left the Court to hold council together.   The men who held Jesus mocked and struck Him, then He was led away. They can do no more till dawn.

MAGDALEN.   And dawn is not far off. (*Turning towards the doorway up* R.)   I go now to learn what they will do with him.

JOHN.   From whom do you expect to hear the decision of the priests ?

(MARY *sits on the stool,* R.)

MAGDALEN.   From the officer of the guard on duty tonight, who is known to me.   I will return when I have any further news.   Come with me, Rachel.

(RACHEL *and* MAGDALEN *go out* R.)

MARY.   Tell me, John, of that last hour in the Garden of Gethsemane, before the soldiers came to arrest Jesus.   Were you with Him ?

JOHN.   Yes, Lady.   When we reached the Garden, Jesus called Peter, James and me to go apart with Him saying, " My soul is exceeding sorrowful unto death." We did not know why he should be so sorrowful. " Wait here and watch and pray," He said, then went apart. We were very weary and lay down. Presently, through the stillness we heard His voice— " Father, all things are possible to Thee " . . . then an anguished cry—"Take away this cup from Me " . . . (*As he crosses to the table.*) Oh! the note of agony in that prayer.

MARY. What is the cup He dreads so much ? O John, is it some cup of sorrow none may share ?

JOHN. Who can tell ? His next words were calm and strong—" Father, if this cup may not pass from Me except I drink it—Thy will be done." Then there was silence in the Garden. In our utter weariness, we fell asleep, and when He came again He found us sleeping. " Could you not watch with Me one hour ? " He said. We were ashamed, but our eyes were heavy with fatigue. Three times He left us to agonise in prayer and returned to find us sleeping.

MARY (*rising*). Oh! My Son! Would that I might have been beside you in that hour.

JOHN. Lady, it was hard to tell you how we failed Him! We are poor tools for the Master's use!

MARY. You are the ones He chose. (*She moves to the window.*)

JOHN. Now I go to Pilate's Judgment Hall to be near the Master.

MARY. God's blessing rest upon you, John.

(JOHN *exits* R. MARY *kneels by the window and remains in prayer.*)

(*The* LIGHTS *dim to Black Out.*)

CURTAIN

Scene II

(GOOD FRIDAY MORNING.)

When the CURTAIN *rises* MARY *is standing by the window.* ANNA *enters* L.

MARY. Greeting, Anna. Have you slept well?

ANNA. Yes indeed, Lady. As I have not slept for twenty years. How can I ever thank you for your goodness to me? For healing my foot, forgiving my wicked words about your son, then giving me shelter for the night. I am more than grateful, Lady. . . . Now I must leave you—so farewell.

MARY Where are you going, Anna?

ANNA. To my daily place on the steps of the Temple, to beg from any who will throw me a coin.

MARY. That is no life for you, Anna, remain with us while we are in Jerusalem, and help us in our daily work—if you would like to.

ANNA. O! Lady that would be joy indeed.

MARY. Then—if you are happy—why should you not return with us to our home at Nazareth?

ANNA. Can you indeed mean it? That such a thing should be possible seems beyond belief. . . . Never needing to beg again—never having to think only of cold and hunger and death. . . . How wonderful!

MARY. You will be very welcome if you will come.

ANNA. Thank you, Lady, thank you with all my heart. Will your son, Jesus, be there too?

MARY. I do not know, Anna. . . . I cannot say.

ANNA. Rachel told me Jesus was a carpenter in Nazareth.

MARY. He was—but He left His carpenter's bench and went out into the world to mend—people. (*She says this with a smile.*)

12

ANNA (*puzzled*). To mend *people*, Lady! How does He do that ?

MARY. He mends broken lives and broken hearts. He heals those who are sick and suffering in mind or body, wherever He goes.

ANNA. How marvellous. How can He do it ?

MARY. By the Power of God. which works through Him. It is a mystery, Anna, which only *He* can understand.

ANNA. And He is your son. . . .

MARY. Yes Anna. Years ago an angel came to tell me of the honour that was to be mine in bearing Him.

ANNA. O! Lady! To think I should have come to *your* door—I—one of the least of all creatures!

MARY. The least may be greatest in the eyes of God. He alone knows the secrets of the heart. . . . You have changed already, Anna. from bitterness. to willing acceptance of your lot.

ANNA (*very quietly*). I have seen Jesus.

(PETER *enters* R.   ANNA *exits* L.)

MARY. Peter, what news do you bring ?

PETER. Lady, they took Jesus from the Court of Caiaphas to be tried before Pilate, by the law of Rome.

MARY. Will Rome prove just, and Pilate deliver Jesus from his enemies ?

PETER. The priests and scribes cried—" He stirs up all the people from Galilee to this place." When Pilate heard the Master was a Galilean, he sent him to Herod.

MARY (*moving down* L.). Have any yet found mercy from that man ? (*She sits on the stool*, L.)

PETER. There is more hope than from the priests and Pharisees.

MARY. Peter, my heart is heavy with foreboding.

PETER. Neither Jewish nor Roman law can condemn an innocent man.

MARY. But he has been fearless in condemning the

Pharisees for their hypocrisy. They are angry and jealous and jealousy is cruel as the grave.

PETER. They cannot bring any accusation against the Master.

MARY. We must wait and hope. *You* are so strong and true, Peter.

PETER (*up* C.). No—No—I am the most unworthy of all His disciples. O Lady, I must tell you. . . .

(*Enter* JUDAS, R.—*he stops in the doorway, seeing* MARY.)

PETER (*exclaiming*). Judas!

MARY (*shrinking back*). Judas—who betrayed my Son!

PETER. Go, Lady. This room cannot hold you and His betrayer—go.

(MARY *rises and exits* L.)

What are you here for, damned traitor ?

JUDAS. I did not know that I should see His Mother, and I thought all the Disciples would be with Him in the Court. (*He crosses to* L. *above the table and picks up a money bag from the floor.*)

PETER. What have you come for ?

JUDAS. The money bag. I dropped it as I left the Upper Room—it is empty.

PETER. You will never carry it again. (*He snatches the bag from* JUDAS.) The Master trusted you with the bag, you stole from it. He trusted your friendship. You have betrayed Him.

JUDAS. Peter, you do not understand the hope I cherished. . . . The hope that Jesus would declare himself a King. (*He comes down* L.) He spoke so often of his Kingdom.

PETER. Did he not say His Kingdom was not of this world ?

JUDAS. I thought that when the moment came, He would assert his power.

PETER. You thought—You thought. (*He comes down to* JUDAS.) What right had you to think beyond what Jesus said? He said He was the Son of God. Was not that title great enough, but you must wish to see Him as an earthly king? You wanted power and riches for yourself. (*He turns away to* R.). We know your love of money. (*A pause. Then he turns sharply to* JUDAS *as a sudden thought strikes him.*) Was there money in your treacherous plan?

JUDAS (*uneasily*). Money! What do you mean?

PETER. Did you sell Him? *Sell* the Master to the priests?

JUDAS. Peter . . .

PETER (*seizing* JUDAS *by the throat*). Answer me. . . .

JUDAS. Let me go.

PETER. Answer then. (*He looses his hold on* JUDAS.)

JUDAS. I wished to compel Jesus to declare His power.

PETER. I have heard that already. Answer my question, or . . .

JUDAS. When the chief priests asked me to lead the soldiers where they might find Him—they did offer me money—

PETER. And you refused it—

JUDAS. I did not see that it could matter if they chose to give it. They said they only wished to question Him and—

PETER (*breaking in with quiet fury*). So you sold Him! Sold the Master!

JUDAS. Peter, you cannot understand. *You* who would never fail Him.

PETER (*arrested in his anger*). Never fail Him. . . . O my God. My God. (*Brokenly.*) I failed Him utterly! (*He turns away up stage.*)

JUDAS. You!

PETER. Yes, I. Though in my pride I swore that I would die with Him, only a few hours later, in the hall of the High Priest, I swore again—denying Him as my Lord! . . . Because they knew and named me as a follower of Jesus—I was afraid. . . . I said I did not know the man! Ah! God! (*He sinks down on to the stool* R. *and drops his head in his hands.*)

JUDAS. Now I remember the Master's words last night in the Upper Room. He said you would deny Him thrice before day dawned.

PETER. *He* knew the weakness of my apparent strength, and since I did that shameful thing I had no right to judge and to condemn! We have both sinned —both failed Him. . . . I repent my rage against you. . . . Forgive me, Judas.

(MARY MAGDALEN *enters* R. *She is in great distress.*)

(*To* MAGDALEN.) Is there any further news ?

MAGDALEN (*coming down* R.). Herod refused to try Jesus and sent Him back to Pilate. Now the priests and Pharisees would force Pilate, against his will, to condemn the Master, and the crowd cried " Crucify Him! Crucify Him! "

PETER (*in horror*). Crucify Him*!* O! God in Heaven!

JUDAS (*wildly*). Crucify Him! No—no—they could not. . . . What have I done! . . . *Crucify Him!* I have sold Him. . . . Sold Him!—for thirty pieces of silver . . . for thirty pieces of silver! (*He breaks down.*)

(*Voices are heard off*—" Crucify Him ! . . . Crucify Him !")

Crucify Him! . . . I will not touch the money, I will throw it back at the accursed priests. . . . God forgive me! . . . No, there can be no forgiveness for such guilt as mine.

(*The cries continue off*—" Crucify Him.")

Crucify Him! I have done this. . . . Master, Master, have pity on my soul.

(*He rushes off* R. *crying.*)

" Crucify—crucify—crucify."

(*Voices off—more distant* " Crucify Him.")

(*Enter* MARY L.)

MARY. What does that cry mean ? Whom do they wish to crucify ?

(*She looks to* PETER *and* MAGDALEN *for a reply, but they are silent.*)

(*After a short pause.*)   I understand.
PETER. Lady, a crowd is fickle. To-day they may cry " Crucify," to-morrow—" Hail! "
MARY. Did not Simeon say, long years ago, a sword should pierce through my soul ? Oh, must it be so sharp a sword as this!

(*Enter* JOHN, *slowly*, R.   *He stands a moment silent, with bowed head at* R.C.)

MAGDALEN. What happened, John, when I had left the Court ?

(JOHN *raises his head and looks appealingly at* MAG-DALEN, *then at* MARY.)

MARY (*realising he brings bad news*). Speak, John.
JOHN (*bowing his head, sorrowing*). Three times Pilate sought to release Jesus and said—" You have brought this man to me as one who perverts the people, but I find no fault in Him, no guilt of the things of which you accuse Him, so I will scourge Him and release Him." But they all cried—"Away with this man, and release Barabbas." Pilate could do nothing in face of that hostile crowd. They had made their choice. He must abide by it.
MAGDALEN. Pilate delivered Jesus to them ?
JOHN (*after a pause*). Yes. . . . (*He looks away.*)

He was scourged first.

PETER. Scourged!

MAGDALEN. Scourged—O! God!

MARY. Is there more to tell ? (*She controls herself by a supreme effort.*)

JOHN. O Lady, must you hear more ?

MARY. I am His Mother, shall I not bear all with Him ?

JOHN. After the scourging, the soldiers led Jesus away to the hall called Praetorium. There they dressed him in a scarlet robe, and crowned Him with a crown of thorns they had plaited, then bowed before Him and mocked Him, crying " Hail, King of the Jews! " . . . Then they spat upon Him and struck Him. . . . He looked on his tormentors with compassion, but never spoke.

PETER. Compassion! How could even *He* find compassion for such men!

MARY. Where is Jesus now ?

JOHN. When I left the Court, they were about to lead Him to the Hill of Calvary. (*In a low distinct voice.*) There they will crucify Jesus.

(*All react to this as the producer may direct.*)

(*A crowd approaching is heard off. After a pause* MAGDALEN *goes up to the window and looks out.*)

MAGDALEN. They come this way. They are already in the street. There is a guard of soldiers behind Him, and on either side a shouting, jeering crowd. The Master is carrying His Cross.

(PETER *has risen and moved up to the window.*)

PETER. It is too heavy and He is weak from torture. . . . Master—Master.

(*He exits quickly* R.   JOHN *goes to the window.*)

MAGDALEN. He stumbles trying to bear the weight. . . . I must follow and be with Him to the end.

(*She exits* R.)

JOHN (*in a heart-broken voice*). He has fallen under it. (*He comes down stage.*)
MARY. My Son! My Son!

(*She exits, followed by* JOHN.)

(*The noise of the crowd grows.*)

SLOW CURTAIN

SCENE III

(EARLY ON EASTER MORNING)

When the CURTAIN *rises* PETER *is standing by the window.* JOHN *is sitting on the stool* L. RACHEL *is standing above the table. She is stirring a jar of spices.*

RACHEL. You are early, Peter.

PETER. I cannot rest or sleep. I am haunted by the memory of my faithlessness. (*He comes down stage* R.) My failure to watch with the Master for one hour. My cowardice in denying Him. Satan indeed possessed my soul.

RACHEL. Why waste time in vain regrets ? You have repented. Now it is *you* who must carry on the Master's work.

PETER. Since he is dead, how can I know what He would have me do ?

RACHEL. The way will be made clear.

(ANNA *enters* L., *carrying a small bowl.*)

ANNA. I heard you say you were going to the tomb of Jesus at daybreak, to anoint His body, and were preparing spices.

RACHEL. Yes, we are going to the sepulchre as soon as the other women come.

ANNA. Do you think I might go with you ?

RACHEL. Yes, Anna, come with us.

ANNA. I bring a little bowl of spices. Yesterday, I sold an ornament of my mother's, it was the only thing I had left. I bought this jar of spices with the money I received.

RACHEL. That was a loving thought.

ANNA. It is only a very small jar.

RACHEL. It is the love, not the size of the gift,

20

Jesus always valued.

ANNA.   Then I may go to His tomb with you ?

RACHEL.   Of course. . . . You will be one of His unknown disciples.

ANNA.   Thank you, Rachel.   Will the other women not mind a beggar being of their company.

RACHEL.   If they did, they would not be true followers of the Master.

ANNA.   Perhaps I might anoint His feet.

(MARY MAGDALEN *enters* R.   *She carries a bowl of ointment.*)

MAGDALEN.   Are you ready, Rachel ?   The other women wait in the street below.

RACHEL.   I am ready and Anna is coming with us, bringing spices.

PETER.   How can you go to the Master's tomb ? The soldiers guarding it will not let you pass.

MAGDALEN.   Why should they not ?   We surely have the right to anoint the body of our dead, as is our custom.

PETER.   Their orders will certainly be to allow none of His followers to approach the place.

MAGDALEN.   I do not fear the soldiers—they *must* let us pass.   Come, let us hasten.

(*She goes out* R. *followed by* RACHEL *and* ANNA. PETER *goes slowly up to the window and stands leaning against the side of it.*)

PETER.   O Master! . . . Guide me.   (*He moves slowly towards the doorway* R.)

(JOHN *raises his head.*)

JOHN.   Where are you going, Peter ?

PETER.   To learn what has become of Judas.   He was mad, I think.

(*He exits* R.   MARY *enters* L.)

MARY (*moving to the window*).   I would watch the beauty of the sunrise.

JOHN.   The sun may rise, for us the world is dark. Jesus was the light of the World—now that Light is quenched.   We walk in darkness.

MARY (*turning*).   John, a moment since, the Cross on Calvary stood out black and stark against the sky, now the sun has turned the wood to gold, and made it as a beacon on the hill.

JOHN.   Light from the Cross on which they killed the Master.

MARY.   Light from the Cross on which He *chose* to die.   Of His own free will He sacrificed His life.

JOHN.   Sacrificed His life! .... (*He rises.*) A light is dawning on what was to all of us a mystery.

MARY.   What was the mystery ?

JOHN.   The words of Jesus and His acts at the last meal we ate together.   He took bread, blest and broke it, and giving it to us, said:—" Take eat, this is My body which is given for you," then passing the cup of wine, He bade us all drink of it, saying " This is my blood, which is shed for many for the remission of sins."

MARY.   His body broken and His blood outpoured. (*She repeats the words reflectively, weighing their implication.*)

JOHN.   That was sacrificial.   I believe Jesus went from that last Supper, knowing He was going forth to die.

MARY.   Offering himself—a willing sacrifice.

JOHN.   For whom ?

MARY.   For those He loved.

JOHN.   He seemed to love all men.

MARY.   Then was His sacrifice offered for all.

JOHN.   Could any be found worthy of such love ?

MARY.   Love does not ask the worthiness of any, but loves for Love's sake alone.   (*She sits on the stool* L.)

(PETER *enters* R.)

PETER. Judas is dead.

JOHN. How did he die ?

PETER. By his own hand. The town is ringing with the story. Overcome with remorse, he went to the High Priests, threw the blood money at their feet, then ran out like a maniac and hanged himself.

JOHN. The world is well rid of such a traitor.

PETER. Poor Judas. (*He moves to the stool* R.)

JOHN. Peter! Can you find pity in your heart for him who betrayed our Master ?

PETER. Who am I to judge any man ? Did I not deny my Lord ? And *He* knew. He knew that I would do it—yet He knelt and washed my feet, while I protested, vowing my loyalty. . . . I couldn't bear to see Him kneel before me as a servant. He so great— I but a rough fisherman.

JOHN. That was the Master's way, teaching us humility by His example.

PETER. True, and so we learned—striving to follow Him with stumbling steps, until the path became too hard, the road too steep, that led to Calvary, and we fell by the way, leaving the Master to face death alone. (*He turns away and goes up stage, then turns and speaks to* MARY.) Lady—Rachel, Mary Magdalen, and other women of our company went to the sepulchre at dawn with spices, to anoint the body of Jesus.

MARY. When they return, I will go to His grave alone.

(MARY MAGDALEN *enters* R.)

MAGDALEN (*crossing quickly to* MARY). O! Lady!

MARY. What has happened ?

MAGDALEN. The sepulchre. . . .

MARY. What of the sepulchre ?

MAGDALEN. It is empty! Jesus is not there. . . . His body is not there!

(PETER *and* JOHN *move quickly towards her.*)

MARY (*rising*).   His body is not there ?

PETER.   What do you mean ?

MAGDALEN.   No soldiers were on guard, the stone was moved away from the entrance to the tomb—the Master's body is gone.

MARY.   Oh, where can they have laid it ? . . . The body of my Son ! . . .

PETER.   We will seek it Lady, but I think the women must have been dreaming.

JOHN.   Let us run to the sepulchre and see for ourselves.

MARY.   Go, go quickly, for His beloved body must be found.

JOHN.   We will hasten, Mother.   I will outrun you, Peter.

(JOHN *and* PETER *go out* R. *quickly*.)

MAGDALEN.   Can the priests have stolen away His body in the night ? . . . Yet why should they ? . . . It would not profit them, and the grave clothes remain, just as He lay in them.

MARY.   The grave clothes are still there ?

MAGDALEN.   Yes, everything is as it was.

MARY.   That is strange.

(RACHEL *enters* R.)

MAGDALEN.   Lady, Rachel will tell you what we saw and heard as we stood at the empty tomb.   I must follow Peter and John to know what can be done. It is not far, so they will soon return.

(*She exits* R. *quickly*.)

MARY.   What could you see or hear since the place was deserted ? (*She sits on the stool* L.)

RACHEL.   Peter and John would not have believed if we had told them what I will now tell you.   But indeed the thing is true.   As we women walked in company to the sepulchre, we wondered how we should move the great stone from before it.   Imagine our astonishment when we came to the place, to see the stone already rolled away, and no guard there. . . . All was still in that hushed hour of dawn, save for the song of a bird.

MARY. Who can have moved the stone and stolen away the body of my Son ?

RACHEL. As we approached, there seemed a strange mysterious sense about the place. Some of our company were afraid and would not go forward, but Mary Magdalen and I went on to the entrance of the sepulchre. There, in the place where Jesus had lain, stood a young man, dressed in a long, white garment. His face shone with unearthly radiance. We were very frightened but he turned to us and said: " Do not be afraid, you seek Jesus of Nazareth who was crucified. He is not here, He is risen."

MARY. " He is risen."

RACHEL. Yes—Those were his words. Can it have been an angel of the Lord who spoke with us ?

MARY (*softly to herself*). He is risen. Most surely an angel brought that message.

RACHEL. How wonderful an angel of the Lord should speak with us.

MARY. There were angels at the birth of Jesus, who brought the news to shepherds in the fields.

· RACHEL. That was a truth that all might see and prove—but that a man can come forth from the tomb where he has lain dead for three days is beyond our understanding. Though we were bidden not to be fearful, we were still afraid and fled, leaving our spices by the empty tomb.

MARY. He will not need them.

(RACHEL *moves up to the window.*)

RACHEL. I see Peter and John, they come running. They have hastened indeed.

(PETER *and* JOHN *enter* R.)

PETER. The thing is true. The Master's body is

not in the tomb.

JOHN. I entered and saw the grave clothes lying, and in that empty place I felt the presence of the Lord Himself. I believe that He is risen from the dead.

MARY (*speaking more to herself than to them*). He *is* risen from the dead.

PETER. Then where is He now ?

(MARY MAGDALEN *enters* R.)

MAGDALEN. Christ is risen! I have seen Him!

MARY (*rising*). You have seen Him!

PETER. Where, when ?

JOHN. His body, or His spirit ?

MAGDALEN. Just as we knew Him, but with the wounds in hands, and feet, and side. . . . As I knelt and wept at the sepulchre, suddenly I felt a presence near, and turned my head away to hide my tears. Then I was aware of a great sense of peace about me, and a voice spoke my name—Mary. It was *His* voice, the voice of Jesus. I trembled with mingled joy and fear then turned and looked up, to meet His eyes. . . . I would have kissed His feet and held them lest He should depart, but He forbade me. " Touch me not," He said—" for I am not yet ascended to my Father and your Father—to my God and your God."

MARY. Did He not say that He would rise again on the third day ?

JOHN. Why were we faithless! Why did we not believe His words ?

MAGDALEN (*to* PETER *and* JOHN). He sent you a message. " Go, tell Peter and the brethren," He said, " that they meet me in Gallilee, whither I go before them."

PETER. He remembered me, who so cruelly failed Him. O Master, Master, was ever love like yours ?

MARY. It is the Love of God. The Love which has destroyed the fear of death.

JOHN. The Cross was not defeat but Victory.

CURTAIN

FURNITURE AND PROPERTY PLOT

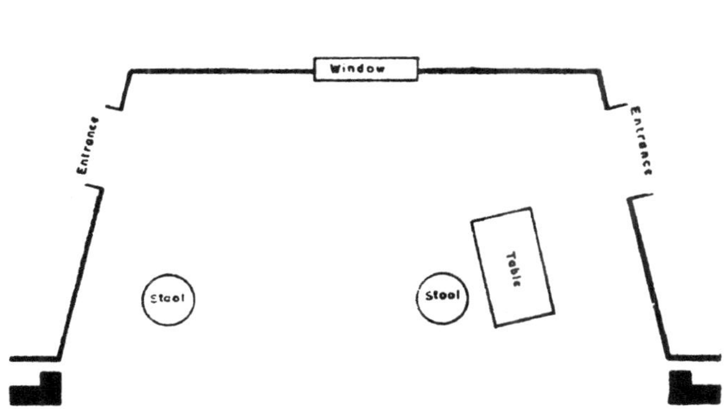

On Stage:

    Table. *On it:* piece of needlework, two small jars (one containing oats).

    Stool, L.

    Stool, R., *beside it:* pestle and mortar.

    On floor above table: money bag.

Off Stage, L.

    Basin (copper, brass or pottery) ⎫

    Sponge (or cloth)   ⎬ RACHEL

    Towel   ⎭

    Jar of spices (RACHEL)

    Jar of spices—very small (ANNA)

Off Stage, R.:

    Jar of spices (MAGDALEN)

www.ingramcontent.com/pod-product-compliance
Ingram Content Group UK Ltd.
Pitfield, Milton Keynes, MK11 3LW, UK
UKHW021820150726
7214IPUK00017B/230